Fostering Children's Faith

Fostering Children's Faith

A Privilege and a Responsibility

Jeanne Hall

RESOURCE *Publications* · Eugene, Oregon

FOSTERING CHILDREN'S FAITH
A Privilege and a Responsibility

Resource Publications
An Imprint of Wipf and Stock Publishers
199 W. 8th Ave., Suite 3
Eugene, OR 97401
www.wipfandstock.com

ISBN 13: 978-1-61097-949-8
Manufactured in the U.S.A.

Dedicated to my husband Gerry
and my sons Jacob and Eli

Contents

Preface

I WAS officially rehired to the position of pastoral assistant for faith formation at St. Catherine of Siena parish in Seattle in September 2011. The rehiring followed a three-year absence during which I had the privilege and challenge of completing my Masters of Arts Degree in Transforming Spirituality at Seattle University and a Certificate in Early Childhood Education through Portland State University. Three months earlier I had unofficially attended a staff meeting where Victoria Ries (St. Catherine's pastoral co-ordinator) brought up the idea of eventually creating a written resource—perhaps several handouts or a short booklet—designed to help support parents in rooting their children in the Catholic faith. Because I was not working or attending school in the summer of 2011, I had time to mull over her suggestion. I found myself strongly drawn to the idea of creating a resource to help parents foster their children's faith. What was initially a potential work assignment swiftly transformed into a very personal endeavor, and one I pursued entirely on my own time.

I entered into the process of creating this book by carefully reflecting on and praying about my experience of fostering children's faith—as a mother, a teacher, and a god-mother. I took time to read books and articles on children's faith formation and child development. I read many, many children's picture books related to faith. As I read, prayed,

ix

and reflected, the two questions that persistently surfaced in me were quite simple and straightforward: What information would have supported me in my efforts to foster my sons' faith? What format and content would be most useful and accessible for parents? Gradually I came to the conclusion that I needed to create a resource on children's faith formation that was well organized, had breadth and depth, and yet was short enough to appeal to busy and sometimes overwhelmed parents. The end product of my prayer, reflection, research, and writing is the book you hold in your hands.

Writing this book has been a deeply satisfying and enriching experience. It has afforded me the opportunity to carefully consider and write about my understanding of faith, spirituality, and the Catholic tradition. It has helped me to integrate and synthesize my experience as a parent, a preschool teacher, and a children's minister with my educational background in human development, early childhood education, theology, and spirituality. As noted earlier, writing this book led me to read many wonderful books and articles on children's faith formation. I found Tom McGrath's book *Raising Faith-Filled Kids* particularly helpful because it clearly articulated an understanding of faith that I hold close in my heart. He eloquently writes that "Faith is a relationship of love with our God played out across the days of our lives."[1] This insight that faith is first and foremost about relationship with God, rather than belief about God, permeates and guides all that is written in this book. I discuss this definition of faith in greater detail in the introduction.

While this book does focus on children's faith formation in the context of the Catholic tradition, I believe much

1. McGrath, *Raising Faith-Filled Kids,* 13.

of the content will have appeal and relevance for a wider Christian audience. Regardless of denominational affiliation, I hope I this book will be helpful to all who seek to foster their children's relationship with our infinitely welcoming and loving God.

Introduction

FOSTERING FAITH in children is a shared privilege and responsibility of parents, godparents, and the church community. Parents, godparents, and the Christian community promise our children at baptism that we will support them in their faith formation. We need to take this promise seriously.

Perhaps it is best to begin by clarifying what I mean when I use the terms religion, spirituality, and faith. They are words that are intimately related to one another and are sometimes used interchangeably. There are many definitions of these words. The definitions I provide reflect the meaning assigned to them throughout this book.

RELIGION

Our religion—our fundamental set of beliefs about the nature of reality and God—is Christianity. Our religious tradition is Roman Catholicism. We are members of the Roman Catholic Church and identify ourselves as being Roman Catholic or simply Catholic. Catholics profess that God is One and God is the Trinity—Father, Son, and Holy Spirit. We believe God loves us beyond all of our imagining. Our tradition is rich in ritual, sacraments, images of God, symbols, theological perspectives, spiritual practices, and a profound commitment to justice and peace. Catholicism understands that all of life is sacramental—all of life is capable of transmitting God's grace. Thus every object in our homes, every relationship, every moment of family life, and any contact with creation can deepen our connection to God.[2]

FAITH

It is important to bear in mind that for Catholics there is always a personal and communal dimension to faith. Faith is sometimes used synonymously with profession of belief. St. Augustine once said, "Faith is to believe what you do not see; the reward of faith is to see what you believe." Faith is often understood to be our willingness to place our trust in God. The word faith can also be used to refer to our religious tradition; Catholics often describe their religion as the Catholic faith. While I agree that profession of belief in God and trust in God are fundamental aspects of faith, in this book I first and foremost recognize faith to be our relationship of love with and in God.[3] Our relationship of love with God (our faith) is grounded in our encounter with God (with Love) in ourselves, in one another, in our faith communities, and in our world. Our faith is nurtured through the community of people in our lives who support our growing understanding and beliefs about God. The deeper our love relationship with God (our faith), the greater our capacity will be to believe and trust in God. As Catholics we are called to live our faith—our relationship with God—in all facets of our daily lives. Our faith formation is ongoing throughout our lives because our relationship with God is always evolving. As Catholics our faith is uniquely shaped

2. McGrath, *Raising Faith–Filled Kids*, 13.

3. Ibid., 4.

by our encounters with God through our experience of the Catholic tradition, of the Catholic faith.

SPIRITUALITY

Spirituality is a word in common parlance in our society these days. For some people spirituality may not be rooted in a religious tradition or a connection to God. But for Catholics, spirituality is always rooted in God. Our spirituality involves awakening to and living into our deepest identity as children of God and followers of Jesus. Spiritual practices support us in awakening and living into who God calls us to be. As Catholics we believe all people are created in the image of God and that our deepest identity can only be discovered in and with God. All meaning in life is rooted in God who calls us to be love in our world.

YOUR HOPES AND DREAMS

Before reading further it might be helpful if you take a moment to reflect on what your hopes and dreams are for your children with regards to the development of their faith, spirituality, and rootedness in the Roman Catholic Church. I will offer many suggestions throughout this booklet to support children's faith formation at home. As you read, notice which suggestions best match your hopes and dreams. These will be the practices to begin introducing and nurturing in your family life.

YOUR FAITH FORMATION

It is important to bear in mind that in order to help foster your children's faith and spirituality, you need to nurture your our own faith and spirituality. We cannot give what we do not have. If you want to root your children in the Catholic faith, you will need to take time to deepen your understanding of our tradition so that you can more fully share it with your children.

As a mother, I understand that parents tend to be very busy and are often under a great deal of stress. Parenting is a rewarding but consuming vocation. The task of juggling parenting and other commitments is a difficult one. Adding another expectation to your "to do" list may seem unwieldy. For this reason it is often wise to begin nurturing your faith formation by taking small manageable steps. Regularly attending Sunday mass, taking a few moments to pray each day, and occasionally participating in adult faith formation opportunities offered at your parish are three significant ways to begin nurturing your faith and spirituality.

1

The Critical Role of Parents

OUR DANCE with God begins the moment we are conceived. God is always with us, always seeking relationship with us, always loving us into being. It is God who leads us and invites us into the dance of life. God has planted a longing for God, for Love, in each of our hearts. Parents have the amazing privilege and responsibility of being "God's love with skin on"[1] for their children. The way parents love and relate to their children day in and day out is the single most powerful influence on their children's faith formation—on the formation of their children's relationship of love with God.[2]

RESPONDING TO CHILDREN'S NEEDS

Loving and nurturing children—physically, emotionally, and spiritually—requires ongoing self-giving on the part of parents. The vocation of parenting challenges parents to faithfully and lovingly respond to their children's needs. Children's needs are many. Children need parents who love them unconditionally and who consistently respond to

1. May et al., *Children Matter*, 153.
2. Ibid.

1

them. They need parents who spend time with them and are truly present to them. They need to be listened to and their opinions valued. Children need parents who recognize and celebrate their unique talents and gifts. They need parents who keep their promises (at least most of the time; no one is perfect). They need parents who are committed to working out their differences in constructive rather than destructive ways—even if parents are in the throes of a painful separation or divorce.

Children need parents who are truthful. They need parents who are trustworthy and reliable. Children's ability to trust their parents provides a strong foundation for the development of their ability to trust God.[3] This is not to say that children who are raised by neglectful or abusive parents cannot learn to trust and love God. The grace of God and the wonder of human resiliency know no bounds.

SETTING LIMITS AND EXPECTATIONS, AND USING POSITIVE DISCIPLINE

It is incredibly helpful for parents to have a good understanding of child development so that they can set appropriate expectations for their children. Please refer to appendix A for a list of books on child development.

Children need parents who provide consistent behavioral limits that balance freedom with protection. In early childhood and throughout adolescence, children need to be allowed to experience logical or natural consequences when they break family rules. Consequences need to be in line with the child's developmental level and should always

3. Ibid., 154.

be implemented with compassion. Punishment should not be the focus; learning the consequences of one's actions should be the focus. Over time children gradually internalize externally imposed limits regarding right and wrong behavior. This internalization of parental and societal behavioral expectations shapes the formation of a child's conscience and evolving ability for moral decision making.[4] Many wonderful books on parenting can assist in the development of positive discipline strategies that support the use of age appropriate behavioral limits as well as the use of logical and natural consequences. Several are listed in appendix A.

It is important for parents to make an effort to regularly notice and comment on children's positive behaviors. The behaviors parents pay most attention to tend to grow. Unfortunately children sometimes receive more attention for their negative behaviors than their positive behaviors. When this happens, negative behaviors often flourish.

SUPPORTING EMOTIONAL REGULATION

Beginning in early childhood and continuing throughout adolescence, children need to be supported in developing emotional regulation. Emotional regulation refers to the ability to be able to name and identify emotions and to be able to respond to them appropriately. Young children often need to be guided in techniques to calm down and soothe themselves when distraught. It is important to reassure children that all feelings are part of being human. Feelings are never bad; it is only how we respond to our feelings that

4. Lieberman, *Emotional Life of the Toddler,* 173.

can be problematic. Children need support in developing ways to creatively manage intense feelings and to develop impulse control. The need to learn skills for managing one's emotions is not limited to childhood; one only needs to encounter road rage on the freeway to realize that many adults are still struggling with regulating their emotions. Without an ability to manage one's emotions effectively and control one's impulses, it is difficult to avoid responding impulsively to one's emotions, which may result in hurting oneself or others. Several resources to support children's emotional regulation are listed in appendix A.

SUPPORTING THE DEVELOPMENT OF EMPATHY AND THE ABILITY TO SHARE

Children are not born with empathy; rather they are born with the potential for empathy. If parents want their children to grow in compassion and develop a strong ethos of service, they need to begin supporting them in developing empathy when they are very young. Preschool age children are naturally self-focused. They need parents and other significant adults in their lives to point out the impact of their actions on others to help them begin to develop empathy. It is vital that parents and other significant adults in their lives model empathy and compassion for them. It is crucial for parents to acknowledge and describe moments when they witness their children's empathy, kindness, and compassion. Again, what parents pay attention to tends to grow.

Children are not born with a natural inclination to share. The ability to share is an emergent ability in children—one that develops as their sense of self and agency emerge. True sharing is rooted in an authentic desire to give to another person from oneself; true sharing cannot be mandated. Parents can and will likely need to insist on turn taking. Parents can and should encourage sharing, but only the child can give freely from a heartfelt desire to give to another. Whenever a child does share, does give freely and generously, parents should acknowledge their action and label it as sharing.

Children will learn much about sharing by witnessing how the adults in their lives share. Parents have the opportunity and responsibility to model for children God's call to share generously not only with family members but also with people who are in great need. Parents need to encourage children to join them in their practice of the virtue of generosity. It is important to remember that there are different ways to give generously—we can give of our time, talent, and/or wealth. It is wonderful to include children in the decision making or discernment process with regards to your particular family's call to generously share with others.

BEING A 'GOOD ENOUGH' PARENT

Children need parents who are "good enough."[5] Whenever parents fail their children (which is inevitable), parents have the opportunity to model humbly acknowledging their failings, asking for forgiveness, and seeking reconciliation. Similarly if parents need support from others for whatever reason, they have an opportunity to model how to graciously ask for and receive help. Every moment we

5. McGrath, *Raising Faith-Filled Kids*, 39.

spend with children is a teachable moment. Humor can be an invaluable asset for parents and their children when the teachable moments are fraught with tension.

Parenting is such a momentous task—perhaps the most important undertaking of a parent's life. Fortunately children do not need perfect parents. Children need parents who are committed to doing their best and loving them extravagantly.

While the faith formation of children is profoundly influenced by how we parent our children in our day-to-day, moment-to-moment interactions with them, intentionally integrating spiritual practices, rituals, service, Bible stories, and symbols into family life will serve to root your children in the wisdom, truth, and beauty of the Catholic faith tradition. The remainder of this book will offer suggestions for fostering Catholic faith formation.

2

Images of God

STUDIES INDICATE that children can begin to form an image of God between the ages of eighteen months and three years.[1] Children construct their image of God from their experience—from what they hear, touch, feel, taste, and see. It is helpful to bear in mind that "children learn what they live. They absorb knowledge of the world by what they experience and observe . . . they learn more from what adults do than from what adults say."[2] This is reminiscent of the wise advice attributed to St. Francis of Assisi: "Preach the Gospel at all times and when necessary use words."

Due to their active imaginations and magical thinking, young children have little trouble believing in a God they cannot see. Many young children—particularly those raised in a Christian faith tradition—tend to assume God is like their parents or other important adults in their lives.[3] The impact of loving parenting on a child's image of God and relationship to God cannot be overstated.

1. May et al., *Children Matter*, 153.
2. Thompson, *Family The Forming Center*, 22.
3. May et al., *Children Matter*, 152–53.

OFFERING A WIDE RANGE OF IMAGES

The dominant language for God in the Catholic tradition is trinitarian. God is one God and God is Father, Son, and Holy Spirit. Even though God is profoundly revealed through trinitarian language, it can be helpful to draw upon a variety of images for our relationship with God. At different points in our life we may be comforted or drawn to certain images and upset or repelled by others. For many young children the image of God as the good shepherd is very powerful and reassuring. Similarly many young children easily relate to the image of God as father. However, if a child (or an adult) has had an experience of an abusive or absent father, imaging God as father may be difficult and unsettling. Fortunately the Bible offers a wide array of images of God from which to draw. Examples include:

- Creator (Gen 1:1)
- Fire (Exod 24:17; Acts 1:3)
- A small still voice (1 Kgs 19:11–13)
- King (Ps 103:19)
- A rock (Ps 95:1)
- Mother (Isa 49:15)
- Counselor (Isa 9:6)
- A potter (Isa 64:6–8)
- Mother bear (Hos 13:8)
- Wisdom (Wis 10:15–17)
- A baby (Matt 1:18–25; Luke 2:1–21)
- A mother hen gathering her chicks (Matt 23:27)

- The good shepherd (John 10:11)

- Light (John 9:5, 14:6)

- The true vine and the vine grower (John 15:1)

- The truth (John 14:6)

- The way (John 14:6)

- The word (John 1:1)

- The sound of wind (Acts 1:2)

- Love (1 John 4:8)

It is best if at least some of the images of God that children encounter visually (in prayer cards, icons, illustrations, etc.) reflect the child's gender and cultural background. Having a culturally relevant image of God may help children enter into relationship with God more easily. It helps them to have a better connection to the idea that they are created in God's image. Several artists who offer diverse images of God include Fr. John Giuliani, Br. Robert Lentz OFM, Br. Michael O'Neil McGrath OSFS, and Julie Lonneman.

CREATING VISIBLE SIGNS IN THE HOME

Objects in our homes are silent witnesses to the sacred.[4] If a stranger walked into your home would he or she see any visible signs that your family is rooted in the Catholic tradition? Would she or he see visible signs of what you value? Would he or she have a sense of how you image God?

4. McGrath, *Raising Faith-Filled Kids*, 75.

Do you have religious symbols such as crucifixes, icons, statues, prayer cards, a blessing cup, a copy of a beloved prayer, etc., in your home? Are they displayed on your walls, shelves, or refrigerator door? Because it tends to be visited so frequently, your refrigerator door is a wonderful place to display copies of prayers, blessings, grace for meals, photos of loved ones, photos of people or situations you are praying for, scripture passages, inspiring words, schedule of church events, etc.[5]

If you do not have symbols from the Catholic tradition in your home, take time to reflect on what symbols you feel drawn towards. What symbols move your heart and help to draw your attention to God? Consider creating or purchasing a few symbols of your faith for your home. Invite your children to participate in the selection or creation of them. Encourage your children to select or create symbols of their faith—their relationship with God—for their bedroom(s). Children can create images of their faith in very simple, cost-effective ways. Here are a few suggestions:

- Invite children to draw and/or paint their image of God. This can be quite illuminating for parents. Who does your child imagine God to be? Your children can tape their pictures on the walls in the bedroom. You may want to frame a picture that your child has spent a great deal of time, effort, and love on.

- Invite children to draw and/or paint a scene from a favorite Bible story.

- Invite children to create a symbol of their faith

5. Ibid., 87.

out of salt dough. Refer to appendix K for the salt dough recipe. One of the most common and simple symbols to make is a cross. Other symbols include a star, an angel, a dove for the Holy Spirit, a cup to represent the chalice at mass, a heart for the love of God, or the early Christian symbol for Christ—the fish—*Ichthys*. *Ichthys* is a Greek word meaning fish but it is also a Greek acronym that translates into Jesus Christ, God's Son, Our Savior. It consists of two arching intersecting lines that create the shape of a fish. It can be easily drawn on a flattened piece of dough.

- Consider creating beeswax candles with your children. Sheets of beeswax and wick are relatively inexpensive. Children tend to love candles and in our faith tradition lit candles symbolize the light of Christ. You might want to light the children's candles during family prayer time.

- If you are a little more ambitious, you could paint a rainbow (with or without your children's help depending on their age) on a wall in their bedroom. The rainbow is an image for God's covenant with Noah and the people of God. Rainbows delight and inspire all of us and are beautiful reminders of God's faithfulness, care, and love.

If you decide to purchase symbols of our faith, children are often drawn to the following images:

- Jesus as the good shepherd

- Jesus welcoming and embracing children
- The Holy Family (Joseph, Mary, and Jesus)
- A nativity set—preferably unbreakable
- Angels
- Icons or pictures of saints children are familiar with or named after
- A cross

As mentioned earlier in this chapter, consider choosing images connected to God that reflect your child's gender and cultural background.

3

Prayer

GOD IS always with us, always loving us into being. Prayer is the practice of taking time to be with God, to turn our attention and hearts towards God who loves us beyond all of our imagining. Our relationship with God, like all intimate relationships, needs time and attention to flourish. Thus prayer is absolutely fundamental to faith formation—to the formation of relationship with God.

Prayer centers our hearts and attention on what is truly most important in life: love. Prayer immerses us in love. Prayer helps us to cultivate and expand our capacity to love. Prayer impacts and shapes each of us in unique and powerful ways. Prayer may foster inner peace, wisdom, generosity, compassion, awe, gratitude, joy, playfulness, a sense of intimacy with God, etc. Prayer is not solely for our benefit. Prayer is a powerful source of love and healing for our world.

Even when prayer feels rote, dry, or unproductive, it has the power to transform us and help us to draw closer to God. God yearns for us to draw closer. God longs to connect with each of us. Whenever we turn to God in prayer, God welcomes and embraces all of who we are in that particular moment: our questions, concerns, anger, grief, anxiety, illnesses, sins, failures, fatigue, boredom, successes, gratitude, wonder, excitement, joy, laughter, etc. God's hospitality for each of us knows no bounds.

While it is essential for parents to take time (if only for a few minutes each day) to pray alone and to pray with their children, it is also vital for parents to pray *for* their children. The prayers of parents are blessings of love for their children. Children need and deserve them.

Establishing and maintaining a practice of prayer requires commitment and persistence. If you are new to prayer, starting a practice of prayer may feel a little intimidating or uncomfortable. It can sometimes feel challenging to set aside a regular time for prayer when our lives are busy and filled with responsibilities. However, the benefits of praying regularly—by ourselves and with our children— are beyond measure.

PRAYING WITH CHILDREN

Taking time to pray regularly with your children is a privilege and a responsibility. The following are a few suggestions for praying with your children at home:

- Choose a regular time for prayer each day—two common choices are dinnertime and bedtime.

- Create a special space in your home for prayer. You and your children may want to create a prayer altar that has a covering that reflects the color of the liturgical season and displays a Bible, crucifix, an icon, art, flowers, a candle, stones, etc.

- If you do not pray in a special location, consider lighting a candle when you pray together.

- Encourage your children to memorize prayers. Repetition facilitates memorization. Memorized prayers can be a great source of comfort in times of crisis. Choose prayers that are important in our Catholic tradition. When your children are preschool age, teach them how to make the sign of the cross and pray the Glory Be, the Hail Mary, and the Lord's Prayer. When they are in first or second grade, introduce the Apostle's Creed and the Prayer of St. Francis. In grades three through five, introduce the Prayer of St. Theresa, the Nicene Creed, and the rosary. Please refer to appendix B for a copy of these prayers.

- Invite your children to pray in silence with you. Encourage your children to be quiet for a few minutes and just sit with you and God.

- Pray prayers of petition—for those in need in your family, in your neighborhood, and in the world. Pray for those who have hurt you or with whom you are in conflict.

- Pray prayers of thanksgiving.

- Reassure your child that they can say anything to God. Reserve judgment and allow them opportunities to express any and all of their feelings to God including anger and doubt.

- Pray the examen at night with your children. This is a prayer form developed by St. Ignatius that can assist us to recognize God's presence in our lives and help us to discern what gives us life and what drains us of life. Regularly practicing the examen can lead to a deeper sense of gratitude for all of the blessings in our lives. Children as young as four can begin to participate in the examen. Refer to appendix C for a description of praying the examen with children.

- Sing with your children. The old adage "to sing is to pray twice" rings true for many people. Please refer to chapter 4 for further discussion on music and prayer.

- Young children need and love to move. Encourage your children to pray to God through movement and dance. Prayer need not always be quiet and serious. Prayer can be active, exuberant, and playful.

- Pray to God through art. Painting, drawing, sculpting, creating collages, writing, etc., become prayer whenever we enter into them with the intention of connecting to God.

- Many people—and certainly children—often intuitively connect with God through experiencing the beauty, diversity, and wonder of creation. When you are outdoors spending time and playing with your children, occasionally give voice to your gratitude to God for the gifts you see and experience: the sparkle and warmth of sand on a beach, the cool refreshing water of a lake, the presence of wildlife, the fragrance and beauty of wildflowers, the intricacy of a spider's web, a grassy hill to roll down, a field to run in, stars to gaze at, the warmth of the sun on your body, etc. Invite your children to voice their appreciation and gratitude for whatever is igniting their awe and wonder.

- Encourage but never force your children's participation in prayer.

4

Music, Media, and Technology

Music can play an invaluable role in fostering faith in children and adults. Music is evocative and can influence our mood and energy levels. Music can comfort or disconcert, excite or calm, inspire or deflate, provoke laughter or tears, stir hope or despair, and so on. Music can provide an outlet for sharing our stories, beliefs, fears, passions, and questions. Music has the power to connect us to our deepest feelings and longings. Music can draw people together; it can help to foster a sense of unity and community. Whenever we participate in music (listening, singing, dancing, or playing an instrument) with the intention of drawing closer to God, music becomes a form of prayer. Music provides a powerful outlet for expressing our feelings, praise, thanksgiving, and lamentation to God.

Music can root itself deeply in our hearts and minds with or without our conscious assent. Music can linger long in our memories, particularly if we are exposed to it often or it becomes linked to strong emotion. Lyrics and melodies of songs learned as very young children are often recalled with relative ease throughout our lives.

Perhaps when we first consider the role of music in faith formation, we tend to think of the music we encounter and take part in at church—the Gloria, the hymns, our sung responses, the Psalms, instrumental music, and Christmas carols. Music used in church is designed to help us draw closer to God. Hymns and sung responses can instill the word of God into our hearts, minds, and bodies. Church music can challenge, inspire, and perhaps even initiate conversion in us. Our active participation in music at church enhances the music's potential to influence us, and it increases the likelihood that we will remember the lyrics and melodies. Many of us who regularly sing at mass may find ourselves humming or singing hymns long after we have left church.

While it is important for parents to sing at mass and to encourage their children to sing at mass, hymns and sacred music need not be limited to church. You may want to intentionally integrate hymns into your everyday lives. You might want to sing hymns for grace at meals, at bedtime, while traveling in the car, or when doing chores.

While listening to and participating in music at church can powerfully inform and transform us, the ability of music to connect us to God stretches far beyond the doors of the church. There is an infinite variety of music that can help us turn our hearts and minds toward God. Examples include music specifically created for children, classical music, jazz, gospel, country, contemporary Christian music, folk, pop, rock, rap, bluegrass, world music, etc. When considering what music might best support your children's development of a loving relationship with God, it might be helpful to consider the following questions:

- What are the lyrics communicating? Do they tell the stories you want your children to remember? Do any teach about Jesus? Are any based on stories from the Bible? Do the songs teach about love, gratitude, and forgiveness? Do they inspire compassion and celebrate acts of kindness? Do they express a wide range of human feelings? Do they encourage friendship, peace, justice, and care for the earth?

- What feelings or overall mood does the music call to mind? Does the music inspire joy and delight? Does it evoke a longing for God, for the transcendent?

- Pay close attention to the songs your children hear on the radio, in movies, and on TV. Are your children inadvertently being exposed to and immersed in music with lyrics that are sexually explicit, filled with violent images, use profane language, or tell stories of revenge, deception, or hopelessness?

Music that inspires, saturates our minds and hearts with its beauty, delights our bodies with its rhythm, speaks of love, stirs compassion, instills peace, tells important stories, generates laughter, gives voice to lamentation, provides an outlet for difficult emotion, etc., has great potential to nurture our connection with God.

Appendix E offers recommendations for recordings of children's music that specifically include content about God and Christianity as well as suggestions for recordings that may not mention God but still convey messages of hope, love, friendship, resiliency, forgiveness, justice, peace, etc.

MONITORING MEDIA AND TECHNOLOGY

It is prudent to be intentional and selective regarding your children's exposure to media and technology. Here are a few questions that may help guide your reflection:

- What forms of media and technology are present in your children's lives? Examples include movies, TV shows, video games, computer games, MP3 players, cell phones, etc.

- If your children watch TV shows and movies, use MP3 players, or play computer or video games, does their experience with them reinforce and reflect your values and the teachings of the Catholic Church?

- Does interaction with media or technology enhance or diminish your children's ability to develop loving relationships with themselves, others, and God?

- What heroes or heroines do you want your children exposed to in the media?

- Does interaction with media or technology limit their active play?

- Do you provide clear guidelines for your children's engagement in media and technology?

- How do you monitor their exposure to media and engagement with technology? (This is more easily done with young children than older children and youth.)

- How are you modeling the use of media and technology? What role do they play in your life?

Media and technology are constantly evolving and emerging. It is important to guide and support your children's engagement with media and technology because their interaction with them has the potential to shape their values, cultivate their images for heroes and heroines, impact their time for and ability to form relationships, and desensitize them to violence.

5

The Sacraments of Baptism, Eucharist, and Reconciliation

THE CATHOLIC faith tradition offers us the incredible gift of seven sacraments—seven amazing possibilities for us to encounter and experience God's expansive hospitality, gracious love, healing presence, and God's call and commissioning of us to be Christ in our world. The seven sacraments include baptism, Eucharist, reconciliation, confirmation, marriage, ordination, and anointing of the sick. In this chapter I focus on the sacraments children most often partake in—baptism, Eucharist, and reconciliation— and their pivotal role in fostering children's loving relationship with God.

BAPTISM

In baptism we are called by name and welcomed as members of the Catholic Church. Our parents, our godparents, and the gathered community promise to guide and support us in our faith formation. We are immersed in the paschal mystery of Christ—in Christ's passion, death, and resurrection. We are filled with the Holy Spirit and are anointed priest, prophet, and king. We are called to be the light of Christ in our world. To support faith formation:

- Celebrate the anniversaries of your children's baptisms and the anniversaries of your baptism. Taking time to remember and honor baptismal anniversaries communicates to your children that you value this sacrament deeply. It provides an opportunity to have a conversation with your children about what it might mean to be anointed priest, prophet, and king. For your celebrations you may want to prepare a special dinner. You may want to light a candle (perhaps your child's baptismal candle) at dinner. You may want to invite your child's godparents to join you for dinner.

EUCHARIST

The word Eucharist means "thanksgiving." All that we have is a gift of God and in the celebration of the Eucharist (the mass) we have a weekly opportunity to give God thanks and praise. As Catholics we believe that God is present to us in very unique and profound ways at the Eucharist: in the word of God, in the consecrated bread and wine—the body and blood of Christ—in the priest, and in the assembly. By coming to the table and being nourished by the Eucharist—by Christ—we are transformed anew into the body of Christ. At the end of each mass we are blessed and sent forth to be Christ in our world.

Children will be invited to prepare for and celebrate First Eucharist when they are in second grade. To support faith formation:

- Eat meals together as a family at least one time a day. Turn off the TV and any other potential sources of distraction. Begin the meal by saying grace together. Allow meals to be a time to talk and listen to one another. Because the Eucharist is a meal, children who share meals regularly with their families will more easily understand that one is nourished body and soul at the table.[1] Refer to appendix D for examples of prayers to use for grace.

- Attend mass on Sundays and holy days as a family. Participate fully in the sung and spoken responses.

- Take time to educate yourself about the Eucharist. Deepening your appreciation of and connection to the gift and mystery of this sacrament will not only support your personal faith formation, it will also enhance your ability to help your children grow in their understanding of and participation in the Eucharist.

- If you feel called to do so, volunteer in ministries at mass—as a lector, a Eucharistic minister, an usher, a leader of children's liturgy of the word, or as a greeter. Call your parish office for information on volunteering for ministries.

1. McGrath, *Raising Faith-Filled Kids*, 93.

- Encourage your children or youth to participate fully at mass by sharing their gifts and talents. Preschool age children can assist parents as greeters or ushers. When children can read fluently and are willing to learn how to proclaim the word of God at mass, many parishes offer opportunities for children to lector occasionally. If there is a children's choir, children can often join the choir when they are in kindergarten. Children in grades five through eight can volunteer as altar servers. Youth in high school can volunteer to lector and cantor at Sunday mass or join the adult choir.

- If your parish offers children's liturgy of the word, children ages four through eleven will be invited to celebrate the liturgy of the word apart from the main assembly. Children will gather with two adult leaders after the opening prayer and return after the prayers of the faithful. Children's liturgy of the word is designed to meet the needs of young children. Fewer readings will be proclaimed and the word of God will be broken open with the active participation of the children.

RECONCILIATION

God calls us to daily "forgive others their trespasses" (Matt 6:14). There are countless opportunities to practice forgiveness and reconciliation in families. Parents and their children are frequently (if not daily) challenged to seek, receive, and grant forgiveness.

Forgiveness is a process. Forgiveness makes demands upon the recipient and the person who forgives.[2] Forgiveness does not involve accepting ongoing injury or abuse. Forgiveness begins by acknowledging the pain and injustice done to us. Forgiveness involves releasing our need to judge the other person, our resentment, and our desire to make the other person pay. Reconciliation is the process of restoring a relationship. In the case of severe or significant abuse, reconciliation may not be the goal. Forgiveness is always our hope and goal.

True forgiveness cannot be forced. Fortunately many of the hurts in families are minor and relatively easy to forgive. If sincerely spoken, the simple words "I am sorry" and "I forgive you" accompanied by a smile, hug, touch, or other comforting gesture can work wonders.[3] Encourage but do not force children to say they are sorry. Insistence on an apology when a child is not contrite forces the child to lie. However, even if a child does not apologize, set clear expectations that he or she needs to make an effort towards restitution or reparation for the wrong done.

Parents need to begin guiding their children in the process of forgiveness when their children are very young. Forgiveness is most effectively taught by a combination of example and instruction. The value of parents modeling the process of both giving and seeking forgiveness cannot be overstated.

We need to be aware that young children under the age of eight may have difficulty telling the truth and sorting fact from wishes or intentions. They may not be able

2. May et al., *Children Matter*, 156.
3. Farrell, *Celebrating Faith*, 76.

to consistently differentiate between an accident and intentional wrong-doing. In fact very young children believe that the intent of the person is not as important as the results of the action.[4] They believe the greater the amount of physical damage, the greater the wrong. Clarity in understanding intentionality may not emerge until middle childhood— sometimes not fully until age ten.[5] Even if they did not intend harm, children still need to make amends for the hurt they caused. We need to support their emerging capacity for empathy by helping them to become aware of the impact of their actions on others. We need to engage children in the process of choosing how to apologize and how best to make restitution.

Regardless of what wrong-doing our children or youth have committed, they need to be reassured of our abiding love and care for them. When children routinely experience forgiveness in their families, they can more easily believe in God's boundless mercy.[6] They need ongoing reminders that God is loving and abundantly merciful. In the Catholic Church we are blessed with the opportunity to regularly receive the words of God's forgiveness at mass and in the sacrament of reconciliation.

Children are invited to prepare for and receive the sacrament of reconciliation when they are in second grade. This sacrament offers us the gift of encounter with God's gracious gift of forgiveness and reconciliation. It offers the wonderful opportunity to hear and receive into our hearts the words of God's forgiveness.

4. May et al., *Children Matter*, 158.

5. Ibid.

6. Farrell, *Celebrating Faith*, 76.

As Catholics we are asked to participate in the sacrament of reconciliation at least one time a year and anytime we have committed a serious sin. We have the option of participating in communal or individual celebrations of the sacrament. Communal celebrations are often offered twice a year—once in Advent and once in Lent. Most parishes have a regular time each week when they offer individual celebrations of the sacrament of reconciliation. To support faith formation:

- It is crucial for you to model partaking in this sacrament as well as encouraging your children's participation. If you want your children to view this sacrament as a gift from God and if you want them to be comfortable participating in the sacrament of reconciliation, it is important to partake in this sacrament more than the minimal one time per year.

- As a family attend your parish's communal celebrations of the sacrament of reconciliation in Advent and Lent.

- Participate in individual celebrations of the sacrament of reconciliation at least once or twice each year.

6

Our Call to Service

ALL OF US—from the youngest to the oldest among us—have unique vocations to love and be of service in our world. As we enter ever more deeply into relationship with God who is Love, Compassion, and Mercy, we are called to deepen our commitment to being sources of love, compassion, and mercy in our world.

CREATING A MODEL OF SERVICE

For many people engaging in service not only grows out of their relationship with God, it builds and strengthens their relationship with God. Engaging in service has great potential to foster and strengthen faith in you and your children.

As parents you have many opportunities to engage in service through loving, caring for, and nurturing your children. Your love and care for your children and your commitment to serving in the wider community provide an ongoing model of loving service for your children. As mentioned previously in this book, modeling is a very powerful means of instruction and motivation for children.

Please refer to appendix F for suggestions for service for children, youth, and families. You may need to try out several different types of service until you and your family discover what best matches your personalities, strengths, interests, and availability.

It is essential for all of us—but particularly for busy parents—to carefully balance self-giving with self-care. Parenting can be a deeply satisfying and joyful vocation, but it can also be stressful and exhausting. As the Quaker theologian Parker Palmer writes, "self-care is never a selfish act—it is simply good stewardship of the only gift I have, the gift I was put on earth to offer to others."[1]

It behooves all of us to recognize that taking time for self-renewal should not be an afterthought but rather a necessary practice for anyone who is committed to being a source of love, compassion, and mercy in our world. The simple truth is that we cannot give what we do not have. To serve others well—including serving our children—we must take time for self-care. If we make time for self-care, we will be modeling for our children something quite wonderful and counter-cultural: a balanced life.

---

1. Palmer, *Let Your Life Speak*, 30.

7

The Importance of Story

THE CATHOLIC Church teaches that God is truly present to us through the proclamation of scripture at mass. As Catholics we are not compelled to believe that the scriptures are literally true, but rather that they reveal the truth. As the Jesuit priest and author Anthony de Mello noted, "The shortest distance between a human being and truth is a story."[1] The stories of our faith tradition from the Hebrew Scriptures and the New Testament are rich vehicles for encountering and experiencing God. They have the power to gift us with wisdom and insight. They challenge us over and over again to more fully devote ourselves to love—of God, neighbor, and ourselves. Regularly setting aside time to read and pray with scriptures (individually or in a group setting) is a powerful way to support adult faith formation.

INTRODUCING THE BIBLE AND SAINTS

As parents you have the privilege and responsibility to introduce stories from the Bible to your children and to encourage them to read and study the Bible throughout their lives. Whenever you share biblical stories with your

1. de Mello, *Anthony de Mello*, 8–9.

children, avoid offering your interpretation of the stories. Instead, invite your children to join you in wondering about the meaning of the stories. Please refer to appendix G for suggestions for scripture passages to read with your children, children's Bibles, and picture book Bible stories.

As Catholics we also place great value on learning from and being inspired by the stories of saints. Please see appendix G for suggestions for picture books on saints as well as reference and chapter books on saints.

BOOKS ABOUT GOD, PRAYER, AND THE CATHOLIC CHURCH

It is helpful to share books with children about God, prayer, and Catholicism. Please refer to appendix G for a list of picture books on these topics.

PICTURE AND CHAPTER BOOKS

Picture books and chapter books that are not explicitly about God, the Bible, saints, prayer, or Catholicism can still be wonderful resources to enrich faith formation. Books offer endless opportunities to explore forgiveness, feelings, relationships, and values. Books can help us to build empathy, introduce us to heroes and heroines, increase our awareness of injustice, inspire a desire to work for peace, introduce us to other cultures and traditions, fill us with hope, move us to tears or laughter, and more. Please refer to appendix H for suggestions for picture and chapter books. The lists of picture books are organized thematically. Some of them will be most appropriate for very young children ages one to three (particularly the board books) and others for children ages four and older. However, it is hard to be age specific about the appeal of picture and chapter books. I recommend that you borrow the books from the public library or an archdiocesan library and read the books yourself before reading them to your children. I trust parents will know which books best meet their children's interests and attention span. The lists given are in no way comprehensive.

FAMILY STORIES

Children need to hear the stories of their family history. The family stories you tell them need to include the unvarnished history of your family.[2] It is reassuring for children to know that they are not the only ones who make mistakes. Stories of resiliency in the face of failure and adversity have great meaning for all of us and certainly for children. Children enjoy hearing about your experiences as a child. Stories that make us laugh are invaluable family treasures. Stories of forgiveness and stories about the lack of forgiveness can provoke great conversations and opportunities for reflection. Stories that deal with sensitive issues such as alcoholism provide opportunities for talking about the dangers of the use of alcohol. (You will, of course, need to use your judgment regarding when to tell the more painful parts of your family story.) It is also important to tell the story of your family's connection with religion and God.

Children need to and love to hear stories about themselves. Children thrive on hearing that they were wanted

2. McGrath, *Raising Faith-Filled Kids*, 223–26.

and loved before they were born or adopted. Children are fascinated by what they were like when they were in the womb and when they were babies. Children are interested in the stories of their birth and baptism. They enjoy hearing funny stories about themselves or stories about good deeds they did. Encourage them to tell their own stories. It is always fascinating and sometimes quite enlightening to hear a family story told from a child's perspective.

Taking time to share stories has the potential to strengthen the relationships between you and your children. Storytelling is a time that allows you to share your values with your children in a very relaxed, fun, and often spontaneous way.

8

Rituals

A RITUAL is simply "a way we do things."[1] It is an action we do over and over in our lives. Whatever we do over and over has the power to profoundly shape us.[2] Rituals provide our lives with rhythm and structure. They often add meaning and depth to our lives. They have the potential to influence and foster our faith, our relationship with our loving God.

THE PURPOSE AND BENEFITS OF RITUALS

The Catholic faith tradition is steeped with ritual. Symbolism and ritual are intrinsic to the celebration of each of the seven sacraments. The sacrament in which Catholics have the most frequent opportunity and privilege to engage in is the celebration of the Eucharist—the mass. In Catholic churches throughout the world, the order of the celebration of the Eucharist is the same: the gathering rite, the liturgy of the word, the liturgy of the Eucharist, and the sending rite. At mass Catholics always sing, pray, give thanks, ask forgiveness, share a sign of peace, are fed at the table of the

1. McGrath, *Raising Faith-Filled Kids*, 88.
2. Ibid., 92.

Lord, receive God's blessing, and are sent forth to be Christ in our world.

As we attend mass regularly, the ritual of the mass seeps into our very being—body, mind, and soul—and becomes a crucial way that we connect with and experience God. The mass can be a source of consolation, stability, and love at any time in our lives, but particularly so when we find ourselves experiencing grief, pain, or turmoil. The predictability of the ritual can be very grounding and reassuring.

Each time we participate in the ritual of the mass we offer our lives to God and open ourselves to receive the power of the Holy Spirit so that we may grow in holiness and be transformed into the body of Christ. We are always commissioned forth from mass to live love, to be love in our world. Love is the source, the focus, and the fruit of the celebration of the Eucharist.

The rituals of the Catholic Church took many, many years to evolve and are continuing to slowly evolve. Similarly, though on a much smaller scale, as our families grow and develop over time, our family rituals gradually evolve. Like the rituals of the Church, the rituals in our families have the power to change and shape us. We may not always be aware of or intentional about our family rituals. Unlike the remarkable consistency of the rituals in the Catholic Church, family rituals tend to be a bit more fluid and changeable because they are impacted and shaped by the sometimes unpredictable ebb and flow of daily life. Still, all of our families have rituals whether we are conscious of them or not. The more consistent our family rituals are, the more powerfully they will shape our lives and our faith. Examples of common family rituals include:

- Kissing our spouse goodbye before we go to work.

- Going out on a date with our spouse on a regular basis.

- Praying—alone or with our children.

- Greeting our children in the morning after they awaken.

- Reading a bedtime story to our children, tucking them in, and telling them we love them before saying goodnight.

- Drinking a warm beverage with breakfast every morning.

- Making a special family breakfast on Saturday mornings.

- Saying grace and eating dinner together.

- Celebrating birthdays.

- Celebrating anniversaries of baptisms.

- Sending valentines on Valentine's Day.

- Making Christmas cookies, decorating a Christmas tree, lighting an Advent wreath, etc.

- Attending church regularly.

- Preparing a dinner for relatives or friends who have had a death in their family.

- Going on vacation together each summer.

What makes a ritual sacred? Love makes a ritual sacred.[3] If the ritual fosters love, it is a sacred ritual, a holy

3. Ibid.

ritual. The sacred rituals of the Catholic Church offer us profound ways to encounter and experience love. So too many of the everyday family rituals listed above provide possibilities for us to encounter and experience love. Clearly some of the examples of family rituals will nurture and inspire love more deeply and frequently than others. However, any and all family rituals that inspire and nurture love—regardless of how seemingly trivial and commonplace they are—are sacred. If kissing our spouse goodbye each day is a demonstration of affection and love, it is a sacred ritual. If taking time each week to go on a date with our spouse nurtures our marriage relationship and strengthens our ties of love, it is a sacred ritual. Regularly praying is always a sacred ritual because prayer by its very nature opens us up to the possibility of deeper connection with love, with God. How we greet our children in the morning, how we say goodnight, how and when we tell our children we love them, sharing meals together, etc., are sacred rituals whenever they nurture and inspire love.

All parents are in a unique position to intentionally develop sacred rituals in everyday family life that foster love—love of God, self, and others. Catholic parents also have the privilege and responsibility to strongly root their children in the Catholic faith tradition and provide their children with many opportunities to be shaped and blessed by Catholic rituals.

9

Liturgical Seasons and Holidays

THE LITURGICAL seasons in the Roman Catholic tradition include Advent, Christmas, ordinary time, Lent, and Easter. The liturgical seasons offer us many opportunities to create sacred rituals with our families that foster our children's faith.

ADVENT

The liturgical year begins the first Sunday in Advent. Advent is the season of the year when we prepare our hearts to receive Christ anew at Christmas. The liturgical color of Advent is purple except for the third week of Advent, which is rose. Purple represents penance and rose joy. Suggestions for family rituals in Advent:

- Make an Advent wreath. See appendix I for information on the Advent wreath.

- Create a ritual for using the Advent wreath at home. It can be as simple as gathering before or after dinner to light the candles and praying a short prayer together or singing "O Come, O Come Emanuel." (The first week you light

one purple candle, the second week two purple
candles, the third week the rose candle and two
purple candles, and the fourth week all of the
candles.)

- Listen to Advent music rather than Christmas
  carols during the season of Advent. Refer to
  appendix E for a few suggestions for Advent
  music.

- Watch a special movie or TV show with your
  children that is connected to the story of Christ's
  birth.

- Set up a nativity set with your children. For young
  children an unbreakable set is best. Encourage
  your young children to play with the figures and
  act out the Christmas story. You may want to
  consider waiting until Christmas Eve to include
  the baby Jesus in the scene.

- Celebrate the feast of St. Nicholas on December
  sixth by reading a story about this beloved
  saint. As a family you may want to follow in the
  footsteps of this saint by practicing an act of
  generosity.[1]

- Develop your own traditions regarding decorating
  the Christmas tree and baking Christmas cookies.

- Take time to reflect on the rampant consumerism
  that often infects this season. Be intentional about
  gift giving. You might want to give gifts that are
  environmentally friendly or locally produced. You

1. Farrell, *Celebrating Faith*, 108.

might want to purchase fair trade products that support just wages for farmers and artisans in countries struggling with poverty.[2] You and your children may want to make some of the gifts that you give.

- If your parish offers opportunities for parishioners to purchase gifts for those who are in need in the local community and you are in a financial position to participate, it is wonderful to include your children in the process of purchasing, wrapping, and delivering the gifts.

- Attend your parish's communal Advent reconciliation service.

CHRISTMAS

Christmas is the season that joyfully celebrates the birth of Christ. The Christmas season begins on Christmas Eve and ends the Monday after the solemnity of the baptism of the Lord. The season of Christmas includes the celebration of Epiphany that commemorates the three wise men's visit to the infant Jesus. The season of Christmas lasts close to two weeks. The liturgical color of Christmas is white and represents purity and joy. Suggestions for family rituals in the Christmas season:

- Attend Christmas Eve or Christmas Day mass with your children. If you have young children you might want to consider going to an early Christmas Eve mass. Older children and youth

2. Ibid., 112.

may enjoy midnight mass on Christmas Eve.

- Sing and listen to Christmas carols.

- Christmas carol in your neighborhood.

- Bless your home on New Year's Day. Please refer to appendix J for examples of house blessings.

ORDINARY TIME

Ordinary time occurs twice a year. The first time is between the end of the Christmas season and the beginning of Lent. The second time is at the end of the Easter season until the beginning of Advent. Many feast days and solemnities occur in ordinary time. The color for ordinary time is green, which symbolizes life and hope. Suggestions for family rituals in ordinary time (you will recognize many of them from suggestions in earlier chapters):

- Cultivate the practice of gratitude by sharing what you are thankful for when you gather for a meal.

- Attend mass each Sunday and on holy days.

- Take time to give thanks and pray each day.

- Pray with your children each day.

- Eat at least one meal together each day.

- Pray grace at meals.

- Regularly engage in service as a family.

- Regularly spend time outdoors as a family and enjoy God's presence in all of creation.

- Take time each day to read with your children.

LENT

Lent lasts for forty days and begins on Ash Wednesday. In Lent we are asked to engage in three traditional forms of penance: prayer, fasting, and almsgiving. Through these spiritual practices we seek conversion of our hearts so that we may more fully follow Jesus. Suggestions for family rituals for Lent:

- Attend an Ash Wednesday service with your children.

- Take time to talk about each person's plan for Lent and your family's plan for Lent. How will you enter into the Lenten disciplines of fasting, almsgiving, and prayer?

- Eat simple meals on Ash Wednesday and Fridays in Lent and donate the money you save to a charity such as the hunger relief rice bowl campaign sponsored by Catholic Relief Services. You might want to consider making Lenten pretzels for one or all of your simple meals. Soft pretzels became part of the strict Lenten fast of Christians by the seventh century (and probably earlier). Please refer to appendix K for information on Lenten pretzels.

- Fasting is an act of self-discipline that helps us to grow in solidarity with those who have less than we do.[3] It may help us to get in touch with our hunger and desire for God. There are many ways to fast. You can fast from unhealthy foods,

3. Ibid., 20.

use of the TV, use of the computer or a particular program on the computer, or use of video games. You can fast from criticism or gossip. You can fast from over-work or over-commitment. It is important to choose a form of fasting that will be meaningful to you.

- As a family commit to performing daily acts of kindness. Talk about the opportunities you have had to share kindness when you gather together at dinner.[4]

- Increase the time you pray together as a family.

- As a family take time for special service projects. Even children as young as two or three can be involved in simple acts of service.

- As a family participate in the evening church services on Holy Thursday and Good Friday.

EASTER

Easter joyfully celebrates the resurrection of Christ. The season of Easter lasts for fifty days; it commences at the Easter Vigil and concludes on Pentecost. The week prior to Easter is called Holy Week and begins with Palm Sunday. Holy Week culminates with the *Triduum* (a Latin word for a three-day period). The Triduum begins the evening of Holy Thursday and ends at evening prayer on Easter Sunday. It includes liturgical celebrations on Holy Thursday, Good

4. Ibid.

Friday, Holy Saturday (the Easter Vigil being the high point of the Triduum), and Easter Sunday.

The liturgical color of the season of Easter is white, symbolizing purity and joy. Red, the color of passion, is used on Palm Sunday and Good Friday. Red, symbolizing fire, is also used on Pentecost Sunday when we celebrate the descent of the Holy Spirit on the apostles. Suggestions for family rituals in the Easter season:

- Attend mass at the Easter Vigil or on Easter Sunday. The Easter Vigil begins at sunset on Holy Saturday and lasts for two to three hours. The timing and the length of the Easter Vigil can be difficult for young children, but it is a wonderfully rich and beautiful service.

- If you color Easter eggs, connect the colorful transformation of the eggs to the transformation and joy that Easter brings to our lives.

- On Pentecost wear red to mass.

10

Closing Comments

Faith—our loving relationship with God—is not something that can be imposed. Faith can, however, be nurtured. The task of fostering children's faith is the privilege and responsibility of parents, godparents, and the church community. Faith will most easily take root in children if it informs their day-to-day lives.[1] Loving your children and providing them with a home where they regularly experience kind but firm guidance, forgiveness, compassion, and encouragement are foundational to your role in fostering your children's faith—in fostering their love, trust, and belief in God.

If you want your children's faith to be strongly rooted in the Catholic tradition, you need to integrate Catholic values, traditions, and spiritual practices into your family life. You also need to become actively involved in a Catholic parish. It is essential to attend mass regularly as a family and to become involved in the life of your church community. It is important for you and your children to participate in faith formation programs offered at church as well as to attend fun community-building social events.

1. McGrath, *Raising Faith-Filled Kids*, 4–12.

It is important to note that rooting your children strongly in the Catholic tradition does not guarantee that they will continue to participate in and embrace the Catholic tradition as adults. However, being rooted in our rich faith tradition does provide a wonderful foundation for their ever-evolving relationship with God who loves them beyond all comprehension and is always with them regardless of the paths they choose to travel and the choices they make.

My prayers are with you as you strive to foster your children's loving relationship with God.

Appendix A

RESOURCES ON CHILDHOOD DEVELOPMENT, POSITIVE DISCIPLINE, EMOTIONAL REGULATION, AND FAITH FORMATION

Resources on Childhood Development, Positive Discipline, and Emotional Regulation

Faber, Adele, and Elaine Mazlish, *How to Talk so Kids Will Listen and Listen so Kids Will Talk*

Goleman, Daniel, *Emotional Intelligence*

Gottman, John, *Raising an Emotionally Intelligent Child: The Heart of Parenting*

Joslin, Karen Renshaw, *Positive Parenting from A to Z*

Lieberman, Alice F., *The Emotional Life of a Toddler*

Medina, John, *Brain Rules for Baby: How to Raise a Smart and Happy Child from Zero to Five*

Nelson, Jane, *Positive Discipline*

Resources for Supporting Spiritual Development and Faith Formation in Children

Berryman, Jerome W., *Godly Play*

Coles, Robert, *The Spiritual Life of Children*

Coulter, Patricia, et al., The *Good Shepherd and the Child: A Joyful Journey*

Farrell, Mary Cronk, *Celebrating Faith: Year Round Activities for Catholic Families*

May, Scottie, et al., *Children Matter*

McGrath, Tom, *Raising Faith-Filled Kids*

Nelson, Gertrude Mueller, *To Dance with God: Family Ritual and Community Celebration*

Ratcliff, Daniel, *Handbook of Preschool Religious Education*

Appendix B

PRAYERS FROM OUR TRADITION

The Glory Be

Glory be to the Father, and to the Son, and to the Holy
    Spirit.
As it was in the beginning, is now, and ever shall be,
    world without end. Amen.

The Lord's Prayer

Our Father, who art in heaven, hallowed be thy name;
thy kingdom come
thy will be done,
on earth as it is in heaven.
Give us this day our daily bread;
and forgive us our trespasses,
as we forgive those who trespass against us;
    and lead us not into temptation,
but deliver us from evil. Amen.

The Hail Mary

Hail Mary, full of grace. Our Lord is with you.

Blessed are you among women, and blessed is the fruit of your womb, Jesus.

Holy Mary, Mother of God, pray for us sinners,

now and at the hour of our death. Amen.

The Apostles' Creed

I believe in God, the Father Almighty, Creator of heaven and earth;

and in Jesus Christ, His only Son Our Lord,
    who was conceived by the Holy Spirit, born of the Virgin Mary,

suffered under Pontius Pilate, was crucified, died, and was buried.
    He descended into hell; on the third day He rose again from the dead;
    He ascended into heaven and is seated at the right hand of God, the Father Almighty;

from there He will come to judge the living and the dead.

I believe in the Holy Spirit,

The Holy Catholic Church,

the communion of saints, the forgiveness of sins,

the resurrection of the body and life everlasting. Amen.

The Nicene Creed

I believe in one God the Father almighty, maker of
heaven and earth

of all things visible and invisible.

And in one Lord Jesus Christ, the Only-begotten Son of
God,

born of the Father before all ages.
God from God, Light from Light, true God from true
God,

begotten, not made, consubstantial with the Father;
through him all things were made.
For us and for our salvation he came down from
heaven

and by the Holy Spirit was incarnate of the Virgin Mary,
and became man.

For our sake He was crucified under Pontius Pilate,

He suffered death and was buried, and rose again on the
third day

in accordance with the Scriptures.

He ascended into heaven and is seated at the right hand
of the Father.

He will come again in glory to judge the living and the
dead.

His kingdom will have no end.

And in the Holy Spirit, the Lord, the giver of life who
proceeds from the Father and the Son,

who with the Father and the Son is adored and glorified,

who has spoken through the prophets;

and in one, holy, catholic, and apostolic church.

I confess one baptism for the forgiveness of sins.

I look forward to the resurrection of the dead

and the life of the world to come. Amen.

Hail Holy Queen

Hail Holy Queen, mother of mercy, hail, our life, our
sweetness and our hope.

To you we cry, children of Eve; to you we send up our
sighs,

mourning and weeping in this land of exile.

Turn, then, most gracious advocate, your eyes of mercy
toward us;

lead us home at last and show us the blessed fruit of
your womb, Jesus;

O clement, O loving, O sweet Virgin Mary. Amen.

A Prayer from St. Theresa of Avila

Christ has no body now but yours. No hands, no feet on
earth but yours.

Yours are the eyes through which Christ looks compassion into the world.

Yours are the feet with which Christ walks to do good.

Yours are the hands with which Christ blesses the world.

Yours are the hands, yours are the feet, yours are the
eyes. You are his body.

Christ has no body now on earth but yours. Amen.

The Prayer of St. Francis

Lord, make me an instrument of your peace.

Where there is hatred, let me sow love;

where there is injury, pardon;

where there is doubt, faith;

where there is despair, hope;

where there is darkness, light;

and where there is sadness, joy.

O Divine Master, grant that I may not so much seek to
be consoled as to console;

to be understood as to understand;

to be loved as to love.

For it is in giving that we receive;

it is in pardoning that we are pardoned;

and it is in dying that we are born to eternal life. Amen

The Rosary

According to tradition, the Blessed Virgin Mary gave Saint Dominic the rosary in an apparition in the thirteenth century. As you pray each decade of the rosary you meditate on one of the mysteries of the rosary. The mysteries of the rosary recall the life of Christ from the annunciation to the resurrection and key moments in the life of his mother Mary. Praying the rosary:

- Begin the rosary with the sign of the cross and the Apostles' Creed.

- On the first bead pray the Lord's Prayer, then three Hail Marys and the Glory Be.

- Choose a particular group of mysteries for your prayer time. Reflect on the first mystery as you pray the first decade of the rosary. Praying a decade includes one Lord's Prayer, ten Hail Marys, and one Glory Be.

- For each ensuing decade you recite the same prayers but reflect on the subsequent mystery.

- At the end of the rosary, pray the Hail Holy Queen, or a prayer of your choosing.

THE MYSTERIES OF THE ROSARY

Joyful mysteries

1. The annunciation
2. The visitation
3. The nativity
4. The presentation of Jesus at the temple
5. The finding of the child Jesus in the temple

Luminous mysteries

1. The baptism of Jesus in the Jordan
2. The wedding at Cana
3. Jesus's proclamation of the kingdom of God
4. The transfiguration
5. The institution of the Eucharist

Sorrowful mysteries

1. The agony in the garden
2. The scourging at the pillar
3. The crowning with thorns
4. Carrying of the cross
5. The crucifixion

Glorious mysteries

1. The resurrection
2. The ascension
3. The descent of the Holy Spirit
4. The assumption of Mary
5. The coronation of Mary

Appendix C

THE EXAMEN

St. Ignatius developed the daily examen. St. Ignatius thought that the examen was a gift that came directly from God, and that God wanted it to be shared as widely as possible. The examen is a practice of prayerful review of one's day that can help us to grow in self-understanding and gratitude. It can help us to perceive God's presence in our lives and discern how we are called to follow God. Here are a few suggestions for praying the examen with your children:

- Consider practicing the examen with your children at bedtime. Children as young as four or five can participate in the examen.

- Take a moment of silence with your children to relax in God's presence and remember God's abiding love for each of you.

- For a few minutes quietly reflect on one of these questions: "For what moment was I most grateful during the day?" or "When did I give or receive love today?" Briefly share your reflections with one another.

- Pause to quietly reflect on one of these questions: "For what was I least grateful today?" or "When was I least able to give and receive love? Why was

it hard?" Briefly share your reflections with one
another.

- Never force participation.
- Keep reflections very short.
- Close with a short prayer.

Sleeping with Bread by Dennis Linn, Sheila Fabricant
Linn, and Matthew Linn is an excellent resource
for helping you deepen your practice of praying the
examen as a family.

Appendix D

GRACE FOR MEALS

Johnny Appleseed

O the Lord is good to me, and so I thank the Lord,
For giving me the things I need the sun, the rain and the
apple seed.
O the Lord is good to me! Amen.

Simple Grace

(Sing to the tune of Frères Jacques)
God our Mother, God our Father,
once again, once again.
We would like to thank you.
We would like to thank you.
Amen. Amen.

Traditional Catholic Grace

Bless us O Lord and these thy gifts
which we are about to receive from thy bounty
through Christ Our Lord. Amen.

Traditional Grace

Thank you for the world so sweet.
Thank you for the food we eat.
Thank you for the birds that sing.
Thank you God for everything. Amen.

Appendix E

MUSIC

Advent Music

Wait with Me: Advent of the Promised Son by Susan Bailey

Advent by Gregorian Singers of Minneapolis, Monte Mason director

Night of Silence by Marty Haugen

We Come Dancing by Marty Haugen and Donna Pena

Children's Music with Overt Connections to God and Christianity

Hi God 1–5 by Carey Landry

Standin' on the Rock by Mike Harrison

Seeds of Faith by Rivers Voice

120 Bible Songs—3 CD collection with lyrics and activities, 2008 Twin Sisters

Shout Praises Kids Gospel, Cornerstone Church, Toledo, Ohio

catholicmusicnetwork.com

Children's music not explicitly connected with
theology but which conveys messages of love,
forgiveness, peace, family, friendship, justice, caring
for the earth, joy, laughter, etc.

I have a Box by Bev Bos, Michael Leeman, and Tom
Hunter

We've Been Waiting for You by Bev Bos, Michael
Leeman, and Tom Hunter

Teaching Peace by Red Grammer

Star Dreamer by Priscilla Herdman

Daydreamer by Priscilla Herdman

Rhythms of Childhood by Ella Jenkins

Gift of the Tortoise by Ladysmith Black Mambazo

Rhythm of the Rocks, a Multicultural Musical Journey by
Marylee and Nancy

Howjadoo by John McCutcheon

Family Garden by John McCutcheon

Four Seasons: Autumn Songs by John McCutcheon

Shakin' It by Parachute Express

Dreamland: World Lullabies and Soothing Music by
Putumayo

Sing Along by Putumayo

World Playground by Putumayo

Hug the Earth by Tickle Tune Typhoon

Appendix F

SERVICE ACTIVITIES FOR CHILDREN AND YOUTH

Many of the suggested service activities for children and youth could be done as a family.

Preschool Age Children

- Make cards for someone who is sick or lonely.
- Help prepare food for someone in need or for a bake sale.
- Help a neighbor or church member with a very simple chore.
- Assist with recycling and composting.
- Assist with greeting at mass.

Primary School Age Children

- Help organize and/or participate in food and clothing drives.
- Assist at food and clothing banks.
- Prepare lunches or other meals for those who are hungry.
- Assist with fund-raising for a cause.

- Assist with community projects to care for the environment.
- Assist with yard work or household chores.
- Begin to explore avenues for advocacy for the oppressed (i.e., letter writing).
- Participate in the children's choir, assist with greeting and ushering at mass, lector at special masses, and serve as an altar server (in grade five).

Middle School Age Youth

- Participate in church-sponsored service learning projects such as week long trips in the summer.
- Participate in advocacy for the oppressed or for a cause (i.e., letter writing or non-violent demonstrations).
- Assist in soup kitchens or food and clothing banks.
- Participate in community projects to care for the environment.
- Volunteer with Special Olympics.
- Assist with children's ministries at church such as babysitting and children's liturgy of the word. Youth in seventh and eighth grade can assist at Vacation Bible School.
- Participate in the children's choir, assist at mass as an altar server, and/or lector at special masses.

High School Age Youth

Youth in high school have an endless range of possibilities available for engaging in service.

- Tutor/mentor younger children.
- Engage in advocacy to promote justice and peace.
- Participate in service immersion trips sponsored by church, school, or community organizations.
- Assist at food or clothing banks or in soup kitchens.
- Participate in community projects to care for the environment.
- Volunteer as youth leaders at Vacation Bible School.
- Volunteer with Special Olympics.
- Assist with children's faith formation ministries including babysitting, children's liturgy of the word, Sunday morning faith formation, sacramental preparation, and whole community gatherings.
- Cantor or lector at mass.
- Participate in the adult choir.
- Participate in or organize fundraising events.

Appendix G

BIBLES, BIBLE STORIES, SCRIPTURE PASSAGES, AND THE LIVES OF THE SAINTS

Not all stories in the Bible are appropriate or understandable for young children. For very young children, picture book Bible stories are an excellent way to begin to introduce the story of salvation history. For children ages one to three, board books or lift-the-flap books are ideal. You might also want to take time to tell stories from the Bible in your own words. You might want to act them out with your children.

Children's Bibles are also good resources for introducing biblical stories to children. Children's Bibles are illustrated, the content is abridged, and the text is often simplified. There is a wide range of children's Bibles available. Many children's Bibles can offer young readers easy access to biblical stories.

As children mature, and certainly by the time they are in third or fourth grade, you may want to begin reading stories directly from the Bible with them. You may want to incorporate reading scripture when you pray with your children. Reading the Sunday scriptures the week before they are proclaimed at mass is often a valuable practice for children and adults.

The lives of the saints provide inspiration and guidance for children and adults. All of us can learn much from the lives of the saints. There are wonderful picture books, chapter books and reference books on the lives of the saints.

Bible Passages to Share with Children

- The story of creation (Gen 1:1–2:4)

- The story of Ruth (Ruth 1–4)

- The annunciation and the birth of Jesus (Luke 1:26–38, 2:4–14, and 2:19–20)

- The story of Zacchaeus (Luke 19: 2–9)

- The mustard seed (Matt 13:31–32)

- The prodigal son (Luke 15:11–24)

- The good Samaritan (Luke 10:25–37)

- The lost sheep (Matt 18: 12–14)

- The sower (Mark 4: 3–9)

- Jesus welcoming and blessing the children (Matt 19:13–15, Mark 10:13–16, Luke 18:15–17)

- The great commandment (Matt 22:37–38)

- Feeding of the five thousand (Mark 6:30–44)

- Healing of ten lepers (Luke 17:11–19)

- Our call to care for others (Matt 25:31–40)

- The last supper (Mark 14:17–25, Matt 26:20–29, Luke 22:7–23)

- The washing of the disciples feet at the last supper (John 13:3–18)

- The road to Emmaus (Luke 24:13–35)

- Pentecost (Acts 2:1–21)
- The early Christian community (Acts 4:32–35)
- God is love (1John 4:7–9)

Children's Bibles

De Paola, Tomie, *My First Bible Stories—board book* (toddlers and preschool age children)

De Paolo, Tomie, *The Tomie de Paolo Book of Bible Stories NIV* (primary school age children)

Chancellor, Deborah, *Children's Everyday Bible* (primary school age children)

Hastings, Selena, *The Children's Bible* (children in grades three and above)

Hendrickson's Publishers, *The Holy Bible for Children NRSV* (middle and high school youth)

Kaufer's Religious Supplies, *Catholic Bible Board Book* (toddlers and preschool age children)

Moroney, Trace, *Lift the Flap Bible* (toddler and pre-school age children)

Tagholm, Sally, *The Children's Bible* (children in grades two and above)

Tutu, Desmond, *Children of God Storybook Bible* (pre-school and primary school age children; features wonderful multi-cultural illustrations)

Picture Book Bible Stories

Bolme, Sarah, *Stories of Jesus* (Baby Bible Board Books)

Bozzuti-Jones, Mark Francisco, *Jesus the Word*

Brett, Jan, *Noah's Ark* (board book)

Davidson, Alice Joyce, *My Good Shepherd* (board book)

De Paola, Tomie, *Mary the Mother of Jesus*

Delvai, Marie-Helene, *Psalms for Young Children*

Gerstein, Mordicai, *Queen Esther the Morning Star*

Getty-Sullivan, Mary Ann, *God Speaks in Feeding Stories*

Haidle, Helen, *What Did Jesus Say and Do? More Wisdom for Young Hearts* (board book)

Josephs, Mary, *Jonah and the Whale* (board book)

Josephs, Mary, *Noah's Ark* (board book)

Koralek, Jenny, *The Moses Basket*

L'Engle, Madelene, *The Glorious Impossible*

Patterson, Katherine, *The Light of the World, the Life of Jesus for Children*

Pinkney, Jerry, *Noah's Ark*

Ross, Lillian Hammer, *Daughters of Eve: Strong Women of the Bible*

Weatherford, Carole Boston, *The Beatitudes: From Slavery to Civil Rights*

Wevdeven, Carol, *Story of Daniel in the Lion's Den* (board book)

Waddell, Martin, *Room for a Little One* (board book)

Picture Books about Saints

Armstrong, Carole, *Lives and Legends of the Saints*

De Paola, Tomie, *St. Patrick Patron Saint of Ireland*

Kaufers's Religious Supplies, *My Favorite Saints Board Book*

Mother Teresa, *Stories Told by Mother Teresa*

Meyer, Jane G., *The Life of St. Bridget the Abbess of Kildare*

Norris, Kathleen, *The Holy Twins: Benedict and Scholastica*

Poole, Josephine, *Joan of Arc*

Stiegemeyer, Julie, *St. Nicholas: The Real Story of the Christmas Legend*

Wildsmith, Brian, *St. Francis*

Chapter or Reference Books about Saints, Heroes, and Heroines

Lentz, Robert, and Edwina Gateley, *Christ in the Margins*

Pochtocki, Ethel, *Once Upon a Time Saints*

Sanderson, Ruth, *Saints Lives and Illuminations*

Self, David, *The Loyola Treasury of Saints: From the Time of Jesus to the Present Day*

Shaw, Maura D., *Ten Amazing People and How They Changed the World*

Wellborn, Amy, *Loyola Kids Book of Heroes: Stories of Catholic Heroes and Saints throughout History*

Encounter the Saints Series (twenty chapter books by many different authors; can be bought individually or collectively)

Picture Books about God, Prayer, and/or Catholicism

Cole, Hana, *Hooray I'm Catholic!*

Delval, Marie-Helene, *Images of God for Young Children*

Goody, Wendy, Veronica Kelly, and Ginny Pruitt, *A Peek into my Church*

Fitch, Florence Mary, *A Book about God*

Hess, Ingrid, *Walk in Peace*

Ladwig, Tim, *Psalm Twenty-Three*

Linn, Matthew, et al., *Making Heart Bread*

Jelenek, Frank, *Journey to the Heart: Centering Prayer for Young Children*

Kushner, Lawrence, and Karen Kushner, *What Does God Look Like?*

MacBeth, Sybil, *Praying with Color, Kids' Edition*

Meehan, Mary SSC, *Heart Talks with Mother God*

Milligan, Bryce, *A World of Prayers*

Nussbaum, Melissa Musick, *My First Holy Communion*

Ramshaw, Gail, *Sunday Morning*

Rylant, Cynthia, *Bless Us All: A Child's Yearbook of Blessings*

Sasso, Sandy Eisenberg, *God In-between*

Sasso, Sandy Eisenberg, *In God's Name*

Swain, Gweneth, *I Wonder as I Wander*

Tutu, Desmond, *God's Dream*

Wilde, Oscar, *The Selfish Giant*

Will, Julianne M., and Kevin Davidson, *Catholic Prayer Book for Children*

Wood, Douglas, *Old Turtle* and *Old Turtle and the Broken Truth*

Chapter Book about Prayer

Roth, Nancy L., *Praying: A Book for Children*

Appendix H

PICTURE AND CHAPTER BOOKS

Books that are not explicitly religious can relay wonderful messages about love, family, belonging, forgiveness, feelings, moral decision making, etc. Reading good books with your children and encouraging them to read good books can support their faith formation and be of invaluable benefit in reinforcing your values.

Picture Books

LOVE, KINDNESS, FAMILY, BELONGING

Brown, Margaret Wise, *The Runaway Bunny*
Carle, Eric, *Does A Kangaroo Have a Mother Too?*
Carle, Eric, *Mister Seahorse*
Carle, Eric, *The Very Quiet Cricket*
Fox, Mem, *Wherever You Are*
Fox, Mem, *Wilfred Gordon McDonald Partridge*
Frazier, Debra, *On the Day You Were Born*
Hennessy, B. G., *Because of You*
Joose, Barbara, *Mama Do You Love Me?*
McBratney, Sam, *Guess How Much I Love You*

McCutcheon, John, *Happy Adoption Day*
Mcghee, Alison, *Someday*
Rylant, Cynthia, *The Stars Will Shine*
Waddell, Martin, *Owl Babies*
Waddell, Martin, *You and Me Little Bear*
Williams, Vera B., *A Chair for My Mother*

LOVING AND ACCEPTING OURSELVES, GROWING AND CHANGING

Baker, Keith, *Who is the Beast?*
Cannon, Janelle, *Stellaluna*
Carle, Eric, *The Very Hungry Caterpillar*
Carlson, Nancy L., *I Like Me*
Dr. Seuss, *Horton Hears a Who*
Henkes, Kevin, *Chrysanthemum*
Rylant, Cynthia, *The Wonderful Happens*
Walsh, Ellen Stoll, *Hop Jump*
Wood, Audrey, *Quick as a Cricket*

FEELINGS

Aliki, *Feelings*
Cain, Janan, *The Way I Feel*
Dr. Seuss, *My Many Colored Days*
Fox, Mem, *Tough Boris*
Freymann, Saxton, *How Are You Peeling?*
Hills, Tad, *Duck and Goose How Are You Feeling?*
Viorst, Judith, *Alexander and the Terrible, Horrible, No Good, Very Bad Day*

FRIENDSHIP, SHARING, GENEROSITY

Burningham, John, *Mr. Gumpy's Outing*
Carle, Eric, *Do You Want to be my Friend?*
Heine, Helme, *Friends*
Hobbie, Holly, *Toot and Puddle*
Keller, Holly, *Help! A Story of Friendship*
Lobel, Arnold, *Frog and Toad*
Pfister, Marcus, *The Rainbow Fish*
Pinkney, Jerry, *The Lion and the Mouse*
Rodgers, Fred, *Making Friends*
Voake, Charlotte, *Ginger*

MAKING GOOD CHOICES AND HELPING OTHERS

(In addition to the books listed, many fairytales and folk-tales are excellent resources for helping children to learn about making good decisions and helping others.)

Callahan, Sheila MacGill, *The Children of Lir*
Lewis, Paul Owen, *Crow Boy*
Marzollo, Jean, *Happy Birthday Martin Luther King, Jr.*
McCann, Michelle, as told to by Luba Tryszynksa-Frederick, *Luba the Angel of Bergen-Belson*
McCloud, Carol, *Have You Filled a Bucket Today: A Guide to Daily Happiness for Kids*
Rand, Gloria, *Baby in a Basket*

Chapter Books for Older Children and Youth:

(In addition to the books listed, many biographies about heroes and heroines are excellent chapter books for older children.)

Alcott, Louisa May, *Little Women*

Bond, Nancy, *A String in the Harp*

Curtis, Christopher Paul, *Bud not Buddy*

Curtis, Christopher Paul, *The Watson's Go to Birmingham*

Cushman, Karen, *Rodzina*

DiCamillo, Kate, *Because of Winn-Dixie*

Easton, Jeanette, *Gandhi, Fighter Without a Sword*

Fleischman, Sid, *The Whipping Boy*

Freedman, Russell, *Eleanor Roosevelt: A Life of Discovery*

George, Jean Craighead, *Julie of the Wolves*

Hamilton, Virginia, *In the Beginning: Creation Stories from around the World*

Hautzig, Esther Rudomin, *The Endless Steppe: Growing up in Siberia*

Hesse, Karen, *Out of the Dust*

Lee, Harper, *To Kill a Mockingbird*

L'Engle, Madelene, *A Ring of Endless Light*

L'Engle, Madelene, *A Wrinkle in Time*

Lewis, C. S., *The Chronicles of Narnia*

Lowry, Lois, *Bless This Mouse*

Montgomery, L. L., *Anne of Green Gables*

Montgomery, L. L., *Anne of Avonlea*

Naylor, Phyllis Reynolds, *Shiloh*

Paulsen, Gary, *Hatchet*

Rowlings, J. K., *The Harry Potter series*

Ryan, Pam Munoz, *Esperanza Rising*

Smucker, Barbara, *Runaway to Freedom: A Story of the Underground Railway*

Speare, Elizabeth George, *The Witch of Blackbird Pond*

Tolkein, J. R. R., *The Hobbit* and *Lord of the Rings*

White, E. B., *Charlotte's Web*

Appendix I

THE ADVENT WREATH

The Advent wreath has long been part of the Catholic tradition. However, the actual origins are uncertain. There is evidence that pre-Christian Germanic peoples used wreaths with lit candles during the cold and dark December days as a sign of their hope and longing for the light and warmth of spring and summer. In Scandinavia during winter, lighted candles were placed around a wheel and prayers were offered to the god of light to lengthen the days and restore warmth.

By the Middle Ages, Christians adapted this tradition and used Advent wreaths as part of their spiritual preparation for Christmas. The light of the candles symbolized the triumph of the light of Christ over darkness. By 1600, both Catholics and Lutherans had developed rituals with the Advent wreath.[1]

The Advent wreath is made with evergreens and four candles. The evergreens symbolize continuous life and the four candles represent the four weeks of Advent. In the first week of Advent a purple candle is lit, the second week two purple candles, the third week two purple candles and the rose candle, and in the fourth week all four candles are lit.

1. Farrell, *Celebrating Faith*, 104–5.

The purple candles symbolize the prayer, penance, and humility with which we prepare for Christmas. The rose candle symbolizes joy. The rose candle is lit on the third Sunday of Advent, *Gaudete* Sunday. *Gaudete* is a Latin word meaning "to rejoice." We rejoice on *Gaudete* Sunday because we have arrived at the midpoint of Advent. Our preparation is now half over and we are close to Christmas. The progressive lighting of the candles reminds us that we are preparing our hearts to receive anew the light of Christ at Christmas.[2]

2. Ibid., 105.

Appendix J

NEW YEAR'S BLESSINGS

The following are two rituals for blessing your home on New Year's Day. They are adapted from New Year's blessings found in *Celebrating Faith: Year-Round Activities for Families* by Mary Cronk Farrell.

Bless Your Home with Water[3]

You will need a bowl of water, and a small evergreen branch.

Gather at your front door. Begin with a moment of silence. Ask one person to read this prayer or all can read it in unison: *Good and gracious God please bless all who enter and leave our home in this coming year. Help us to remember you are always with us, always welcoming us, always loving us. Help us to create a home that overflows with hospitality, kindness, forgiveness, and love. Amen.*

Dip the branch in the water and sprinkle the door. Walk through your home sprinkling water and offering a blessing in each room by praying: *Dear God please bless our (name of the room). Help us to remember you are always with us, always loving us. Please help us to love one another and to be sources of love in our world. Amen.*

3. Ibid., 5–6.

Take turns sprinkling and praying the blessing. You may
include whatever rooms and spaces in your home
that you would like to bless. When you have finished,
spend a few moments of quiet together. Close with
a prayer of thanksgiving. Enjoy a special snack
together.

Bless Your Home with Light[4]

You may want to perform this blessing after sunset; you
may want to dim the light in your home. You will
need a candle with a holder to catch dripping wax.
Gather at the front door of your home. Begin with a
moment of silence. Light the candle. Ask someone to
read this prayer or all can read it in unison: *Good and
gracious God, please fill our home and our hearts with
the light and warmth of your love. Bless all who enter
and leave our home this year. Help us to be sources of
light, love, forgiveness, and peace in our world. We give
thanks for our home, our family, our friends, and all of
the blessings in our lives. Amen.*

Slowly walk throughout your home carrying the candle
and shining its light in each room. You may want to
do this in silence or you may want to sing Christmas
carols and/or hymns. Suggestions for Christmas
carols include: "Joy to the World," "We Three Kings,"
"Deck the Halls," and "The First Noel." Suggestions
for hymns include: "Amazing Grace," "Christ be our
Light," "Peace is Flowing like a River," and "This Little
Light of Mine."

Close with a moment of silence. Blow out the candle.

Enjoy a special snack together.

4. Ibid., 6–7.

Appendix K

LENTEN PRETZELS AND SALT DOUGH

Lenten Pretzels

By the seventh century (and probably earlier) many Christians kept a strict fast during Lent as a means of penance and self-denial in preparation for the celebration of Easter. Bread was a major component of their Lenten diet. In that era Christians often crossed their arms when they prayed. Tradition has it that in the seventh century a monk in Italy began to twist simple bread dough into shapes that resembled crossed arms to help remind Christians to be faithful not only to their Lenten fast, but also to their practice of prayer. The twisted bread was called *bracellae*, the Latin word for "little arms." From this Latin term it is thought that Germanic people coined the term "bretzel" which over time evolved to "pretzel."[5]

WHOLE WHEAT PRETZEL RECIPE

1 package rapid rising yeast

1 ½ cups warm water

2 ½ cups white flour

5. Farrell, *Celebrating Faith*, 24.

2 tsp sugar

½ tsp salt

1 ½ cups whole wheat flour

2–3 T of vegetable oil or melted butter

2 T coarse salt or sesame seeds

Dissolve yeast in warm water in large bowl. Add white flour, sugar, and ½ tsp salt. Beat on low speed until moistened. Beat on medium speed, scraping bowl occasionally, for 3 minutes. Stir in enough whole wheat flour to make dough easy to handle. Turn dough onto a lightly floured surface. Knead until smooth and elastic, about 5 minutes. Grease a large bowl with butter or vegetable oil. Place kneaded dough in the greased bowl and then turn the dough over so that the dough is greased on both sides. Cover the dough with a towel and let rise in a warm place until double in size. This should take 45 to 60 minutes.

Heat oven to 425 degrees. Punch down dough and divide into halves. Cut each half into 6 equal pieces. Roll each piece into a rope 15 inches long. Place rope on greased cookie sheet. Bring left end of rope over to the middle of the rope to form a loop. Bring right end of rope up and over the firsts loop to form a pretzel shape. Arrange pretzels about 3 inches apart on the cookie sheet.

Brush vegetable oil or melted butter over the pretzels and spring with coarse salt or sesame seeds. Bake pretzels until brown—about 15 to 20 minutes. Cool on wire rack. Serve with mustard if desired. This recipe makes twelve pretzels.

Salt Dough

Salt dough is inexpensive and easy to make. Children can use salt dough to create a wide range of Christian symbols including a cross, a star, an angel, a dove, a cup to represent the chalice at mass, a heart, a fish, etc. Rolling pins and cookie cutters are useful tools for working with salt dough.

SALT DOUGH RECIPE

2 cups flour
1 cup salt
1 cup water
1 T vegetable oil

Mix dry ingredients together. Mix water and oil into dry ingredients until it forms a soft dough. Move dough to a floured surface and knead for 10 minutes until dough has a smooth and elastic texture. Place dough on a floured surface to make shapes. Bake shapes for four hours in a 200-degree oven or air dry for forty-eight hours. After shapes are cooled they can be painted with child friendly acrylic, tempera, or watercolor paints.

Bibliography

Berryman, Jerome. *Godly Play*. San Francisco: HarperSanFrancisco, 1991.

Campbell, Jim. *52 Ways to Talk with Your Kids about Faith Formation*. Chicago: Loyola Press, 2007.

Coles, Robert. *The Spiritual Life of Children*. Boston: Houghton Mifflin, 1990.

Crary, Elizabeth. *Love and Limits*. Seattle: Parenting Press, 1994.

de Mello, Anthony. *Anthony de Mello: Writings*. Maryknoll, NY: Orbis Books, 1999.

Farrell, Mary Cronk. *Celebrating Faith: Year-round Activities for Catholic Families*. Cincinnati, OH: St. Anthony Messenger Press, 2005.

Gottman, John. *Raising an Emotionally Intelligent Child*. New York: Fireside, 1997.

Johnson, Elizabeth. *Quest for the Living God*. New York: Continuum International, 2007.

Lieberman, Alice. *The Emotional Life of the Toddler*. New York: The Free Press, 1993.

Linn, Dennis, et al. *Sleeping with Bread*. New York: Paulist Press, 1994.

May, Scottie, et al. *Children Matter*. Grand Rapids, MI: Eerdmans, 2005.

McGrath, Tom. *Raising Faith-Filled Kids*. Chicago: Loyola Press, 2000.

Medina, John. *Brain Rules for Baby*. Seattle: Pear Press, 2010.

Nelson, Gertrude Mueller. *To Dance with God: Family Ritual and Community Celebration*. New York: Paulist Press, 1986.

Palmer, Parker. *Let Your Life Speak*. San Francisco: Jossey-Bass, 1999.

Ratcliff, Daniel, ed. *Children's Spirituality: Christian Perspectives Research and Application*. Eugene, OR: Cascade, 2004.

Thompson, Marjorie. *Family the Forming Center*. Nashville: Upper Room, 1996.